HOW TO BE A MEDIUM

HOW TO
BE A
MEDIUM

by

J. Donald Walters

THE AQUARIAN PRESS

This edition 1990
First published as *How To Be a Channel* in 1987 by
Crystal Clarity, Publishers, Fratellanza della Gioia,
Cassella Postale # 48, 1-06088 Santa Maria degli
Angeli, Assisi (PG) Italy. Phone: 011-39-742-811-212.

British Library Cataloguing in Publication Data

Walters, J. Donald.
How to be a medium.
1. Spiritualism
I. Title
133.9

ISBN 0-85030-964-6

*The Aquarian Press is part of the Thorsons
Publishing Group, Wellingborough,
Northamptonshire, NN8 2RQ, England*

Printed in Great Britain by William Collins, Sons &
Co. Ltd, Glasgow

1 3 5 7 9 10 8 6 4 2

PUBLISHER'S NOTE

'Channelling', a term you will encounter throughout this book, is the modern equivalent of 'mediumship', in which people act as a *medium* or *channel* for contact with the spiritual world, and thus the two words may be considered synonymous.

May this book serve
as a channel for Thy Truth.
Amen.

CONTENTS

_____

CHAPTER ONE

A GREAT MODERN CHANNEL

I had the good fortune to live for three and a half years with one of the greatest channels of our times.

He was not widely known as a channel, perhaps because he didn't need to go into unconsciousness, nor into any abstract mental state, to give utterance to what came through him. He simply 'tuned in', and the answers were always there.

And the answers were right. They worked for people. His counselling revealed deep, intuitive insight into the problems, motives, and secret thoughts that people had thought they'd tucked away where no one would ever reach them.

He saw things in people's past that even they had forgotten. He saw far back in time, also beyond the portals of this life, and helped people thereby to understand problems in the present lifetime that, until then, had left them confused, perplexed, or resentful.

And he saw things in their future, as well. People couldn't bring themselves to believe all the predictions he made, but they proved right nonetheless.

He spoke — from personal, visionary experience, and not from book learning — of countless mysteries of the universe: of how it was made, and why. He told us of life on other planets, and predicted a time of inter-stellar travel — which he said was a reality, despite its seeming impossibility, according to the known laws of modern physics.

He described — again, from direct experience — levels of reality that are much too subtle to be perceived by the physical senses.

He spoke of the ages of civilization on earth, and of the implications for mankind of having entered, as we now have, a new age.

He revealed to our imagination a divine creation so marvellous, so infinitely vast and complex, so inspiring in its beauty and lofty purpose that I think not all the books in the world could equal what we heard from him in person.

And yet, he was not generally known as a channel.

He could see people in the astral world, converse with them, receive messages from them. He could tune in to high souls and let them speak through him. From what he told us, and from what seemed to us truly our own experience with him, God Himself used his voice to teach us and guide us.

And yet — there was nothing ritualistic about his channelling, nothing portentous, nothing to make us feel that we had the rare blessing of being given ringside seats at some special and extraordinary event. He was so natural in everything he said, so unaffected, so seemingly casual, that, not infrequently, his most amazing statements almost passed un-noticed — only to be remembered later on with awe.

He never required special circumstances to do his channelling, nor any special environment. I never saw him lie back, close his eyes, and offer up his mind and body to be used as an instrument by another entity, while remaining personally unaware of everything that was being said through him. His channelling came to him as effortlessly as did breathing.

He didn't take on a new personality, or succession of personalities. Normally, his voice never changed while channelling — though there were a few rare exceptions. Never did it assume the tones of someone speaking as if from afar, or unaccustomed to human company, nor did it labour ponderously over the syntax of human speech.

What he channelled, moreover, was never spoken condescendingly. I never heard him fuse expressions such as, 'You people of earth', or, 'As you would say in your parlance' — as though mentally to dissociate himself from the rest of us.

On the other hand, whatever came through him was spoken with dignity, for he himself was a man of dignity. There was no frivolous attempt to descend to our mental level in order to establish a bond of communication with us.

Finally, and most important, he never created a situation where we were forced to go to him for any insights we received. He constantly urged us to go within, to receive the answers we sought in our own inner silence — to become channels ourselves, instead of depending outwardly on another.

This man was a saint. Indeed, he was a master, for he had realized God. His channelling was the result of his constant inner communication with God, as well as with other great saints, who, like him, had merged their consciousness in God.

This man's name was Paramhansa Yogananda.

As a great master, Yogananda is well known to spiritual seekers throughout the world — even behind the iron curtain. He is also regarded with the deepest respect, love, and admiration by other saints and recognized spiritual leaders in many lands.

I became his disciple in 1948, and lived with him until his passing in 1952. Since his passing I have remained with him in spirit and discipleship. I have taught in many countries, and written many books to further his early mission. And I can say without hesitation that his presence has continued to guide, teach, and inspire me inwardly.

I am writing this book to help people understand more fully what channelling means, because I see that there is some confusion on the point in people's minds. Some people seem to think that anyone who sits back, closes his eyes, and allows words to pour out of him without his conscious control may well be acting as a channel for some higher power, and may well be able also to channel some special message personally from that high power to them.

Yet I have seen people hurt and confused by such messages, too. They have been misled in fundamental matters — such as what they ought to do with their lives, or what path they ought to follow in some undertaking that is important to them.

I have known them to be encouraged to develop talents they did not possess, or discouraged from activities that would have furthered their spiritual development.

I have known them to be fed ego-balm — assurances, for example, that they have a glorious future before them, or that they have lived equally glorious lives in their past, often as someone of historic fame.

Rarely, if ever, have I known them to receive the discipline they needed for their present spiritual welfare. Usually, they were treated as though their most trivial questions and spiritually immature perceptions or attitudes were as worthy of grave consideration by the high entity whose words were being channelled to them as any matter concerning people's very spiritual life.

Worst of all, I have seen them become dependent on such channels rather than independent in themselves, and inclined rather to seek outside themselves for their answers than seek them, as all great masters have said we should do, in the silence within.

There is something entirely vicarious about receiving truths, however beautiful, that touch only the mind. That is why great masters, if they have felt divinely led to help humanity, have incarnated here on earth in human form — that they might touch not only human minds, but also human hearts and souls.

CHAPTER TWO

THE STAGES OF CREATION

Paramhansa Yogananda explained that the astral world exists behind — that is to say, on a subtler level of manifestation than — the grosser atoms of this physical universe.

There are, he said, three major stages of manifestation in creation. When God moved His consciousness to create, His first manifestation was in the form of pure thoughts. This level of creation Yogananda likened to an architect's blueprint, which is necessary for the final construction of a building. This stage of divine manifestation is known by great masters as the casual, or ideational, universe.

When God was satisfied with the blueprint

He had projected, He vibrated more grossly the thoughts of which it was composed, and they took on the appearance of light and energy. This level of manifestation Yogananda likened to the activity involved in constructing a building. At this stage of construction, creativity is still in a relatively fluid stage. Changes can still be made, and new ideas introduced without drastically affecting the project.

The universe of light and energy that is the second stage of divine manifestation is called by great masters the astral world, or — more aptly, for those who can visualize its immensity — the astral universe.

The third, and last, major stage of divine manifestation is this physical universe in which we live. To complete Yogananda's analogy, matter is the finished building.

Our physical universe reveals its descent from subtler levels of manifestation. The atoms initially formed only gaseous clouds in space. Eventually these atoms, widely dispersed initially, united to produce stars. The fiery matter of which stars are composed then condensed further, here and there, to produce planets. And planets, molten in their initial state, cooled gradually and became solid like our earth.

The more a material substance cools, the more physically substantial it becomes. Water freezes. Even gases become liquefied. The 'frozen' atoms that form the planets combine to produce individual, solid-seeming physical objects: the rocks, the mountains and continents. A wooden chair seems hard to us when we sit on it. The tree from which it was made seems not only solid, but heavy enough to crush us under its weight, if it should fall.

Our physical bodies, too, seem to us firm and heavy. So engrossed are we in the seeming realities of the material world that even our thoughts often seem to us heavy; and our energy, instead of lifting us higher as it should, often seems weighted down by fatigue.

In actual reality, however, the atoms composing the physical universe are insubstantial, and in a constant state of vibration. The matter composing our physical bodies, so astronomers tell us, may well have formed part of other universes, even of other living bodies in universes that pre-existed the one in which we now live.

Physicists tell us, moreover, that the material atoms are really only manifestations of energy. It is even, they say, perfectly feasible

— theoretically, at least — to withdraw the atoms from their manifestation as a loaf of bread, and to remanifest them as an orange — or as a gold coin. So we see that the physical sciences have already, in this new age, touched the hem of subtler-than-material realities. The astral world seems more real to us than it could have a century ago. And the claims of the ancient alchemists begin to seem not so far-fetched after all.

Indeed, there is the story of a saint of our own times in India who would manifest money whenever he wanted to help others.

The governmental authorities of the area, becoming suspicious, sent a pair of policemen to investigate.

'Where is your printing press?' they loudly demanded.

'Come with me,' the saint replied with calm unconcern. He led them to a large lake nearby, and pointed down into its depths.

'You mean you want us to believe you keep a press down there, in the water?' they shouted. 'Are you trying to make fools of us?'

'Look, I'll show you,' said the saint. Diving into the lake, he emerged a few moments later, smiling, with his hands full of bank notes.

The authorities, utterly bewildered and certainly outmatched, decided they had better drop the case!

When God created our souls, He projected us, too, in three major stages of manifestation. First, He encased us in bodies of thought; ideational, or causal, bodies. This causal body is our innermost reality as manifested beings. It is at this level that the soul comes into manifested existence. (Before that, it is simply a part of the infinite consciousness of God.)

Around this collection of divine ideas, and projected outward from it, is the astral body. Our astral bodies are made of light and energy, just like the astral world.

Projected outward from the astral body, finally, and encasing it, so to speak, is the physical body.

Each successive body is a projection of the subtler body which it manifests. It also, therefore, in certain ways resembles that body. The astral body is an expression, on a level of light and energy, of the ideational body. And the physical body, in a crude, material way, resembles the astral body.

As matter becomes denser, the further it is projected outward from its essential spiritual state, so also with the consciousness of man.

The more our consciousness becomes identified with matter, the more dense, unimaginative and uncreative we become.

Matter hardens as it cools. So, too, with the feelings of the human heart as our capacity for affection cools. Indeed, so also with human consciousness as a whole. For as our interest in the world around us 'cools' — that is to say, as we contract mentally instead of expanding to embrace the challenges of life — our habits become fixed and unchangeable, our ideas harden into dogmas, and we become quite simply — to use Yogananda's colourful expression — 'psychological antiques'.

Man's very body is a replica of the stages of divine manifestation into matter. It contains, deep in the spine, certain *chakras* (as the yogis of India call them): centres, or vortices of energy and consciousness.

The more a person lives inwardly in his higher centres, the more he becomes identified with his own higher nature. His consciousness soars, and expands effortlessly to embrace other people and other realities than his own.

The more, conversely, he lives in the lower centres of the spine, the more he finds himself identified with his lower nature. His consciousness sinks. His mind grows dull. He finds himself contracting inward upon himself, in ever-more-insistent affirmation of his ego, of his separateness from others, and of his own selfish needs.

The languages of mankind reveal that there is a certain awareness of these truths in everyone. People everywhere speak of feeling high or low; uplifted or dejected; of rising or sinking; of having their 'ups and downs' — or '*alti e bassi*,' as they say in Italian.

It actually helps, if one is feeling 'low', to raise one's energy-level by concentrating on the higher centres — especially on the heart centre, which is located in the spine opposite the physical heart; or on the 'Christ centre' in the forehead between the two eyebrows. It helps also, if one wants to progress spiritually, to maintain one's mental focus always at one or the other of these two centres.

All of us form an integral part of God's vast creative process. And as we must evolve back to Him, so must His entire universe.

There are whole galaxies that manifest varying degrees of refinement in the rays of energy they project. At the blazing heart of every galaxy is its divine centre. From that point, rays of light and consciousness flow outward, nourishing the spiritual life of its entire system.

Some galaxies – those that are the least evolved spiritually – are deeply materialistic in the rays of energy and consciousness they project outward from their centre. The majority of beings on the planets in these galaxies are absorbed in selfishness and egotism. Dull in their awareness, their imagination is tied down to gross matter, and is incapable of soaring much above what they see around them already.

The creativity of the people on these planets is at a minimum. They are unable to create high civilizations. They produce no sensitive art, no beautiful handicrafts, no lofty music or poetry. Instead, they exist in a state of unceasing violence, warfare, cunning, and suspicion. Happiness is a state of mind virtually unknown to them. Their lives are relatively short. Illness and disease of all kinds are rampant.

Other galaxies, more developed spiritually, emanate outward from their centre rays of consciousness that are more attuned to the truth that matter is only a manifestation of energy.

The majority of beings on the planets in these galaxies are still matter-bound. (After all, we are still dealing with this grossest universe, the material.) They are more energetic, however, more aware, more creatively active than the inhabitants of the lowest galaxies. It comes naturally to the intelligent beings on these higher planets to create beautiful objects — graceful buildings, sensitive carvings, paintings — and to see energy, even thought itself, as a means of changing and controlling matter.

These inhabitants produce high civilizations, and live, relative to those on the darkest planes, more habitually in a state of peace, of good health, and of general well-being. Egotism and selfishness, though still powerful motivators in human behaviour, are less insistent in their demands. Warfare, consequently, is less frequent — though, when it does occur, its violence is unfortunately the greater for the fact that man, at this stage of his evolution, has so much more power at his command.

Those material galaxies which are the most highly evolved emanate rays of a more uplifted consciousness. The intelligent beings who live on the planets of these galaxies, instead of viewing energy as a means of manipulating and controlling matter — as those do on lower levels of evolution — see matter rather as a portal to entry into subtler, astral realms. These inhabitants live in effortless communication with angelic beings. Their lives are in constant harmony with nature, and with the pure nature spirits which bring life, order and beauty to this physical world.

The creativity of these inhabitants is directed not so much toward creating beautiful forms as toward achieving beautiful states of awareness. Whatever they create materially, however, is effortlessly beautiful, graceful, and beneficial to themselves and to others. These people have little need to construct grand edifices, or even sturdy homes. They 'prefer the shelter of trees,' — as the great master Babaji, one of Yogananda's teachers, once put it — for nature herself becomes temperate when mankind projects thoughts of love and harmony.

Happiness and physical well-being are normal to such planets, though the tensions of material existence are not entirely absent, nor are the emotions that are born of a degree, however slight, of matter-attachment.

Differences are quickly resolved, however, and for the most part loving. Ego-consciousness exists, for its roots are in the astral body, but men's egos are more naturally inclined to reach out to others, and to include their happiness in their own.

The whole universe sings with life! Astronomers have discussed learnedly the possibility of other planets supporting life similar to our own. A few have actually computed the probability at virtually zero!

Such is not at all how the masters have seen God's universe in their deep vision of the infinite mysteries. Countless planets there are, so they tell us, and endless numbers of them are fairly teeming with life. It doesn't necessarily follow, however, that the life on all those planets has the same carbon basis as our own.

People do not remain as inhabitants of one planet forever. Nor do they continuously inhabit only one galaxy. During their long upward journey of evolution through matter, they incarnate on many planets, and in many galaxies.

Nor is progress imposed on them. Each has the free will to progress at his own pace. He may, for instance, incarnate from a moderately evolved planet, or galaxy, to one that is less evolved, if his conscious choice has been to live even more fully identified with his ego, and besotted by matter-attachment. On the other hand, he may leap upward to a much higher sphere of material existence, if his choice has been to live in true harmony with others and with nature.

Planets rarely contain inhabitants who are wholly one type or another. Indeed, people themselves are rarely so composed! Matter doesn't offer the clear differentiation of vibrations that, as we shall see later on, exists in the astral universe. Saints and sinners rub shoulders on the material plane, and that very fact offers people everywhere a major incentive to follow the one example, and avoid the other. For saintly people manifestly radiate happiness, while people of low consciousness are uniformly unhappy.

It is the majority consciousness that determines whether a planet or galaxy is what might be called 'heavy' (that of the lowest type), 'ego-active' (that of medium evolution), or 'light' (that of the highest type).

Once all the inhabitants of a planet have learned the spiritual lessons that are inherently to be learned from matter, the planet itself, having served its evolutionary purpose, is therefore dissolved back into the astral energy of which it was ever simply a manifestation.

One other circumstance exists also under which a planet is dissolved, or destroyed: when its inhabitants become uniformly dark in their consciousness, blind to spiritual realities, and lost in egotism and sin.

Our own planet, as also our galaxy, is at neither end of the spiritual spectrum. It belongs to the middle category, the *ego-active* — that of partial awakening from material delusion. The majority of people on this planet are so engrossed in ego-motivated pursuits as to give only token attention to spiritual truths. They view even those higher realities, moreover, in terms of their material usefulness to them.

Our own solar system, moreover, is situated near the outskirts of our galaxy. The rays of spiritual energy emanating from our galactic centre reach this solar system only faintly, compared to what those systems receive which are closer in.

Living where we do, we have yet far to go in order to manifest our full potential as inhabitants of an *ego-active* galaxy. The majority of people on our earth are, indeed, still strongly materialistic and ego-motivated. Many more on this planet, moreover, than might be were our planet more evolved, are not merely *ego-active*, but *heavy* types, intensely attached to violence, to violent feelings and emotions, and to matter itself as the only reality in which they can believe.

Fortunately, this solar system is presently moving toward our galactic centre. Yogananda gave this as the reason we have entered a new age — not the age of Aquarius, as so many claim, but a much greater leap forward in evolution: into a time when mankind generally will be much more spiritually aware, and will understand, progressively more deeply, the realities of energy and how those realities may be applied to matter.

We are only at the beginning of this age of Dwapara, as it is called. The fact that we have only entered it recently explains the enormous tension that presently exists between old and new ways of looking at things.

As our solar system approaches ever closer to the galactic centre, the new age — Dwapara Yuga to give it its full name — will be bringing much deeper divine awareness to human consciousness than has been seen in history. With this deepening awareness will come a deeper sense of harmony with nature.

It is partly due to the stronger rays of spiritual energy that are already affecting our planet that so many people today are interested in subtler levels of reality, including the astral world, and in channelling information from the astral world to this material plane.

It is important, therefore, for them not to become sidetracked from their spiritual evolution by misinformation as to certain spiritual realities.

CHAPTER THREE

THE ASTRAL WORLD

The physical world is a pale imitation of the astral — a projection of it, but into a grosser medium, rather as if one were to print a brilliantly coloured oil painting onto dull, cheap-quality paper.

One may well wonder why people remain attached to the copy, when they can have the original. The same is true, indeed, all the way down the scale of cosmic manifestation: why remain attached to any of it, when one can have God?

And that is what all the saints ask themselves, once they have found God! All comparisons between the bliss of communion with Him and the second-hand pleasures of

His creation are absurd. God is, as the Indian Scriptures declare, 'supremely relishable'!

Unfortunately, the power of delusion is strong. Nor is it easy to relinquish the known for the unknown. And this, ultimately, is the sacrifice the soul is called on to make. 'He who shall lose his life,' said Jesus,, 'shall find it.'

Why do people cling to matter, when they can have so much greater beauty in the astral world? Basically, because it isn't only the appreciation of beauty that they want. For one thing, they want not only to appreciate it, but to *own* it. And in that thought of ownership they want to protect it, to keep others from taking it and owning it themselves. Their possessive attitude toward things loses the fluidity that is an essential feature of the subtler energy world.

For another thing, people who are attached to matter are afraid of energy: afraid of dynamism, its challenge, its very fluidity. They *like* their fixed habits, fixed mental attitudes, fixed personality traits, fixed ideas and dogmas. Many of them feel more threatened by challenges than enlivened by them. Moreover, instead of embracing dynamic solutions to their problems, they opt for solutions that promise to keep things as little changed as possible. And rather than seek ways to expand their consciousness, they do their best to confine it — even going to the extent of blunting their perceptions, whether through drink, or through drugs, or merely through absent-mindedness.

Physical comfort and convenience are more important to most people than beauty. If they go on a picnic to the countryside, they may think nothing of leaving their garbage behind them by a beautiful stream. If they go on an outing to the beach, rather than enjoy the peaceful roll of the surf they may carry their own little neatly packaged world of sound with them in the form of a transistor radio, which they think nothing of inflicting on the sensibilities of everyone around them.

The pleasures of this physical world are relatively gross, but that seems to be the way people like 'em! And that is why they keep coming back here, until their grosser attachments have been worked out and released. Were they to be given a day in paradise, most of them would feel like a fish out of water, gasping to get back to an environment they can relate to comfortably.

Many of them, indeed, were they to go to

paradise, would soon be desperate for someone to fight with, or argue with, or criticize, or blow up at in a fit of temper. Surrounded by peaceful smiles and friendly understanding, they'd soon feel they were going mad!

Well, then, why don't at least those people whose consciousness I have classed as 'light' leave this physical plane and remain in the astral? As it happens, they do, and ever more so, the more they diminish their material attachments. Their difficulty is simply that vestigial traces of material attachment have a way of continuing to lurk in the subconscious, in dark, hidden corners of memory. It takes time to ferret them all out and bring them up into the light of present understanding, where they will wither and die.

Desire directs energy. And energy directed from the heart pulls us along with it. We return to this plane of existence as long as there is the slightest vestige of desire for what matter alone can offer us. As these vestiges become fewer, and as our sense of identity with the astral world becomes stronger, our sojourns there may grow progressively longer. Alternatively, we may elect to come back quickly with a view to cleansing ourselves as soon as possible of every lingering material attachment.

The only people who return to this physical plane under no personal compulsion of desire are those who come back here to help others in their struggle to achieve freedom from material desires.

People of 'light' consciousness carry astral memories with them back to this physical plane. That is why they try to recreate — usually without realizing the connection — the beauty and harmony they knew there. They give the world beautiful music; beautiful paintings; beautiful landscapes and gardens with gay flowers, trees and broad, soaring vistas, harmoniously designed buildings.

Art that denies beauty in the name of truth and realism merely affirms a lower reality, and rejects a higher for a lower consciousness, preferring ego-bondage to soul freedom.

The astral world of so many people's memories and fantasies is a real place. It is not rock solid, like this earth. For that matter, though, neither are the rocks of our earth at all as solid as they seem. In their atomic structure, the atomic particles are located as far from one another, relatively speaking, as the stars in outer space.

The astral universe is composed of light and energy, but its inhabitants walk about on its planets, just as we do. The flowery meadows are as real to them as ours are to us. In a sense, indeed, they are more real, for the perceptions of astral beings are not dulled by material heaviness. They are free to soar and expand. Consequently, they are much more intense.

The astral universe is much vaster than our own — incredibly vast though this physical universe seems to us! Unlike this universe, moreover, there are no dead planets. Manifestly, on the astral plane, the expression of life and consciousness is the one, true purpose of God's creation. This is His purpose as well on the material plane, but here it is less obviously so.

All things in the astral world, being composed of light, shine with their own light. In the physical world, objects give off colour and beauty only with the light they reflect. Earth colours are therefore dull; their beauty is dimmed.

Not so in the astral world. Beauty of all kinds there is thrillingly beautiful. Colours exist such as cannot be imagined here on earth. The sounds of music strike not only the outer ear, but seem to strike chords in one's entire being. Fragrances are more exquisite than any wafted to us by jasmine or rose. Tastes are like a thousand delicious earthly tastes crushed into one. The sense of touch is an intuitive revelling in streams of radiant light.

Flowery meadows there are in cheerful abundance, pleasant to sit in, and never cold, damp, or beetle populated. Refreshing streams flow gently though verdant fields, never posing a threat to life. High mountains soar majestically, and are scaled, or even flown over, with ease, for in the astral world weight such as we know it on earth doesn't exist. Rainbow waterfalls rush gaily over mountain precipices. Rocks on the upper slopes give way gradually to luxuriant grass in the valleys below, and to stately trees, some of them in full and glorious flower.

The inhabitants' dwellings are graceful, artistic and never subject to the disintegration, rot, or ruin that we know on earth. Communities live together in peace and harmony, and in love for one another and for God. They gladly share their enjoyments, their labours, and their efforts to understand ever more deeply the mysteries of life.

The astral universe is not only much vaster than our own, it is also far more varied. Matter's density prevents it from expressing, except dully, the beauties of that world of light, but it also prevents it from expressing — again, except dully — the astral world's darker side.

For the heaven I have described is the ideal to which mankind may aspire, but not the reality as it is lived by all astral beings. There are heavens far higher and more beautiful than any that can be described in words. And there are also regions far darker than would seem possible here on earth.

For in a world of which the essence is light, an absence of that light is oppressive in a sense that cannot be easily grasped in earthly terms. We might compare it, inadequately, to the emptiness one might experience in this world were there an insufficiency of matter to give anything real substance. In the lower astral regions, similarly, there is a constant sense of lack; of reaching out and not being able to grasp; of helpless rage, frustration and pain.

The inhabitants of these regions, like those in the less evolved regions of the physical universe, know no peace — only discord, hatred and warfare. They experience perennial regret over what they can never have, or over what cannot be changed.

Darkness, like a dull mist, hangs heavily over tired plains and barren valleys. Because the inhabitants' feelings here, as in the higher regions, are intensified by their freedom from bondage to matter, their mystery is far deeper than it would be on earth, where mankind has the capacity at least to dull his mind to suffering.

Inhabitants of the higher regions have the freedom to descend into these dusky hells. They go there with the purpose of helping those whose suffering has brought them to the point of desiring to reach upward, however tentatively, toward the light. For, eventually, these wretched souls inevitably tire of dwelling on the past injustices done to them (for that is how they see the wrongs they themselves have committed). Once they begin to accept personal responsibility for their sorry plight, they begin also to realize that, by changing themselves, they can assume responsibility for altering their condition. It is at this point only that the angels can help them.

Inhabitants of the various regions cannot ascend to higher regions. Thus, merely to be an inhabitant of the astral world doesn't necessarily endow one with higher wisdom than one has already. One may live there and be convinced that there are no angels, no such things as saints and masters, no such reality as spiritual evolution, no such thing in their own future as a return to earth.

Many earth dwellers who, at death, pass on to the astral world are, in fact, even less fully aware than they were here. Having lived on earth in total identification with their physical senses, they haven't developed the intuition to perceive the subtler realities of the astral world. Whatever emotions they experience are intense, but are like the emotions one sometimes feels in dreams: strong, but never brought into clear focus.

When a person dies, he leaves his physical shell behind him. This, however, is only the outermost of his three bodies. He retains his astral body, and, within that, his causal body. Physical death, then, does not mean that one merges into a great sea of energy or consciousness, as so many people nowadays believe. That destiny awaits us in fact — but not, as they insist, in eternal unconsciousness, and not upon the mere act of leaving the physical body. Rather, it comes with release from all the three bodies. It is a conscious self-expansion into the Infinite, into complete oneness with God. This is the state which Jesus, and all great masters, has attained. Conscious liberation from all the three bodies is the esoteric meaning of the Biblical description of Jesus as 'the first begotten of the dead'. (Revelation 1:5)

To the extent that people are conscious of the afterworld, they retain their personalities. A gangster after death doesn't become an angel. He retains his rapacious nature, and suffers for it.

Most people, however, are not vicious. Not always well-meaning, perhaps, their selfishness usually is yet due more to ignorance than ill will. Such souls do not suffer after death — except, perhaps, in the sense of feeling bewildered and disoriented. After a rest in the astral world, their earthly desires draw them back to the material plane in new physical bodies, refreshed and prepared to cope once again with the challenges of earth in their long climb out of the marshes of earthly attachment.

People who have lived good lives on earth

very much enjoy their astral sojourn. This is particularly true if their time on earth has been spent in expanding their mental horizons, their interests, and above all their sympathies towards others, instead of remaining merely entrenched in narrow definitions of goodness.

Such people go to planets with vibrations similar to their own, and there mix with others who share their interests. There is none of the disadvantage, on these planets, of the wide disparity of people that one finds thrown together here on earth.

For each astral planet has its own special vibrations. A planet of musicians will not attract such types as stock market manipulators. Peace-loving people are able to move about freely without fear of being mugged. Those who have a strong sense of family will be united with their family members after death. Those for whom science is their great love will find themselves living among scientists. And those who love the arts will find themselves among artists. The matter is simply settled: like attracts like in the astral world.

Old age and disease, as we know them, are absent from these spheres. Old age, there, is seen rather in terms of spiritual maturity, of wisdom, and not of decrepitude. And disease is primarily dis-ease: the discomfort of feeling out of tune, inwardly. People who, when they die, are attracted to such planets reclaim the bodies, with greatly increased vigour, of their youth on earth.

Those persons whose intuition has been somewhat developed, through regular spiritual practices — especially through meditation — and through striving while on earth to serve as channels for higher guidance and inspiration, are attracted to relatively high astral planets after death. There, they mix freely with angelic beings and with others, more developed than they, who can help them further in their spiritual quest.

Spiritual development, however, is not easy to achieve in the astral world, so long as one remains still bound by earthly desires. The life there is without earth's incentives. It is too beautiful, too harmonious, too deeply satisfying. Lacking are the contrasts we have on earth — the slums that sprawl beside marble palaces; the injustices of the privileged classes to the underprivileged; the seemingly undeserved suffering of good people — all of which drive one forward in one's spiritual evolution with the thought, 'There *must* be a better world!' Unless one has developed deep love for God, he is apt, in the other world, to postpone his spiritual quest.

For this very reason, many souls elect to return as soon as possible to earth — not impelled by any urgency of worldly desire, but simply drawn by the resolution to finish up all desires. Spiritual progress is easier in the physical world. From this plane it is possible to rise even beyond those heavens, and to attain spheres where the inhabitants live constantly in the bliss of God. On those planes, indeed, spiritual progress is not difficult, but is as natural as breathing!

Earth-liberated beings can move about freely in the astral universe. They effortlessly recognize loved ones from past lives, and happily renew past associations, long buried under sands of forgetfulness.

Paramhansa Yogananda, in his spiritual classic, *Autobiography of a Yogi*, gives a wonderful description of the astral universe, and touches on many points that have been left out here, going on to describe the soul's further progress, after the attainment of liberation from earth, as it ascends through higher astral spheres to the causal world, and thence on to final liberation in God.

Inhabitants of the astral world have no difficulty observing our activities on earth. Relatives may come to us in dreams to express their love to us — or, perhaps, to warn us, in the event of an impending calamity in our lives.

Angels roam the streets of man. They inspire with uplifting thoughts and beautiful ideas those whose minds and hearts are open to them. They inspire scientists in their search for new discoveries for the benefit of mankind. They suggest inspiration to artists who long to express truth and beauty through painting, or music, or literature, in order that others, through their works, might achieve more understanding and joy in their lives.

They suggest to sincere truth seekers answers to their deep questions about life and the universe, and to the problem of how to grow in understanding.

The angels also suggest thoughts of comfort to people who grieve. Their thoughts get through, however, only if those people, in their grief, keep their hearts open, and do not reject any help, or enclose themselves within narrow walls of self-preoccupation.

Angels visit hospitals to give strength and comfort to those who suffer physically. Sometimes, they heal those for whom the doctors have abandoned all hope. Often, they help to ease the dying in their struggles to win release from their physical bodies.

Angels roam the battlefields in time of war, soothing the minds of the wounded — sometimes healing their bodies. They usher the dying forth from their pain-wracked physical cages.

If, in war, a case is righteous, they may suggest to the leaders inspirations for achieving victory.

Angels are obliged ever to respect the free will of those whom they would help. They can enter only where they are welcome — perhaps not always by conscious invitation, but at least by a mind kept open, uplifted, and ever searching.

Their response must in some way be drawn. And they respond most readily to positive thoughts, to thoughts full of light, faith, and courage.

Here is a true story, illustrating how they respond to courage, and to the refusal to abandon hope even when all hope seems futile:

A European friend of mine, in his youth, was a mountaineer. As such, he made a number of first ascensions.

One day, he decided to try climbing the side of a mountain that no one had ever tried climbing before. Ascent by the other faces was relatively easy, but this side seemed impossible. Nevertheless, studying it at length, he though he could make it.

He had almost reached the top, when he came to a ledge, above which the mountain swept outward, over the valley. To climb any further would have meant being drawn away from the mountainside by the force of gravity. The task was manifestly hopeless.

Equally hopeless, however, was the descent. It had been an almost impossible climb up to this point. To return the way he had come would be quite impossible.

'Shall I sit here and starve to death?' he asked himself. 'Even though I know I can't possibly go any further, I might as well die trying as die of starvation!'

He started to climb. At the point where the curve of the mountain began its sweep outward, he fell back onto the ledge. Though bruised, he was determined not to give up. He climbed again — and again — and again!

On about the twentieth try, as he once again reached the point where a fall was inevitable — suddenly he was held against the mountain face! He continued his climb. Still he was held.

At last he reached the top of the mountain, and from that point was able quite easily to walk down. Later, he would often tell people, 'The mountain held me to her bosom.' But it was the angels who had held him there!

Astral beings have other reasons for reaching out to the people on earth. One is the desire of earthbound souls to experience, before their allotted time, the pleasures of the material world.

Another is a desire for power. For power is particularly a temptation in the astral world, even as consciousness-deadening activities are the major temptations here on this physical plane.

So you see, not all channelling is equally beneficial!

It is important, therefore, to realize that much of your spiritual development depends on the right kind of channelling. Obviously, then, it is important to learn what is the right kind of channelling, and moreover how to serve your fellow beings on earth as a channel of light.

CHAPTER FOUR

WHAT IS CHANNELLING?

What is channelling?

Simply put: *Channelling is the transmitting of inspiration received from a source other than the ego.*

This inspiration can be of many kinds; it doesn't take only the form of words. Often it finds expression in music, in painting, or in the form of healing energy — to name only three of the best known types of channelling.

Moreover, channelling needn't necessarily be divine. People can also be channels for lower entities, and sometimes even channels for dark ones.

There are two ways to receive channelled inspiration. One is passive; the other, magnetic.

Passive receptivity, also, occurs in two different ways. In one of these, the thoughts are blanked out, and the mind is simply held open to be used as a channel, in the trust that whatever comes through it will be good.

In the second form of passive receptivity, there may be no conscious effort to blank out the thoughts, but there nevertheless will be a kind of blankness: the over-susceptibility of a weak will. Astral entities may find it easy to gain control of such a person. Indeed, possession is more common than is generally realized. Possession is a factor to consider, especially when treating the insane.

Magnetic channelling is the result of a magnetic appeal, offered with full consciousness, and with the strong initiative of the will, on a vibrational level similar to that of the inspiration it receives. An example of this sort of magnetic appeal is what Jesus called 'prayer, believing'.

Another example is the courage my mountaineering friend showed in exerting his own will to the utmost to reach the mountaintop. It was his courage that attracted the help he needed to succeed.

Magnetic channelling is the power displayed by a true healer; it is drawn to him by his compassion for the ill. Such channelling is displayed even more perfectly by a saint, as he allows divine grace to flow to others by his own upliftment in grace.

Magnetic channelling always occurs as a result of some conscious magnetic appeal. One may not consciously realize that he has ever sent out such an appeal. It may even seem to him that what is being channelled through him has been imposed on him without his conscious desire — possibly without his consent! But it seems so only because in opening oneself to a higher power, one also invites the operation of a wisdom greater than one's own.

Thus, prayer is sometimes answered in ways very different from what we originally asked, or perhaps even wanted. Time, in such cases, however, always reveals that the answer given us was the best — in fact the only right one for us and for our own and others' true happiness.

Such unrecognized magnetic attraction exists, for example, in the case of one who receives healing powers without having thought to ask for them. The gift is given him purely because of his compassion for others in pain.

Such unrecognized attraction exists also in the case of a person who receives a poem or a song, perhaps even while thinking of something else. He seems not to have asked for the inspiration. And yet, there will certainly have been *something* in his attitude that invited the inspiration. He must at least have some deep inclination towards music, in order to attract true inspiration in the form of music. He must love poetry, in order to receive a beautiful poem — as opposed to the sort of doggerel that might come to a prize fighter.

One little-known aspect of this subject is that the magnetic appeal, and the conscious preparation that makes it possible for one to become a channel, may have taken place in a prior life.

A case in point is that of the three children at Fatima, Portugal, who received miraculous visions of the Virgin Mary, followed by a channelling of world prophecies and a number of amazing miracles.

Another case is that of Bernadette Soubirous, to whom the Virgin Mary appeared at Massabielle, outside Lourdes, France. At the end of those appearances there appeared the miraculous spring, in the waters of which countless people have since been healed.

None of those children actively sought the divine experiences he or she received. Many biographers, indeed, have described them as perfectly normal children in every way, though probably their motive for doing so was primarily to discourage anyone from thinking the children abnormal. Otherwise, no one has ever suggested that they were in any way *un*worthy of the graces they received. And all agree that they were exceptionally pure in heart and mind.

We may assume that there was a magnetic appeal in their very purity, born of who knows how many devotional practices in the past. It was this quality, surely, that drew to them the graces they received.

For divine grace flows only into those channels where it has been invited to come. To do otherwise would be to flout the most fundamental principle of divine law: the right of every intelligent being to the exercise of his own free will.

Thus, a peasant may receive the divine guidance to lead an army. Far from inviting such guidance, he may even reject it — at least at first. And yet he may go on to become one of the famous generals of history. Such was the story of St Joan of Arc.

A mechanic may suddenly receive the inspiration to write beautiful music. Or an unlettered person may receive deep insights into the Scriptures. Always, in such cases, there will have been a period of preparation in prior lives — as well as, in this life, eventual recognition of the fitness of that which has been received.

What, then, of passive channelling? This sort of channelling is simply never the way high souls are attracted to mankind. All great masters have spoken unequivocally on this point.

Think of it this way: would a person of any refinement enter a house merely because it was there, and the door happened to be open? A door wide open with no one standing in it, smiling, extends no warm, loving invitation. It would be an act of sheer presumption to take advantage of such an opening to come in and snoop about.

The angels' deepest desire, where mankind is concerned, is to help those of us who are in need. We must each, however, reach out consciously for help, first. Otherwise, the angels would feel that it was a presumption to intrude.

Well, then, but might an angelic being use a person whose mind was passively opened to receive him, provided *others* issued a magnetic appeal to him to appear in this way?

Astral beings have been know to do so, but never angels. And never masters. Highly evolved souls know that it is against every divine principle to *use* anyone!

The offering of one person at an altar by a congregation of worshippers, with the prayer that he be used as a channel by their deity, was quite possibly the original meaning of human sacrifice. One person, usually a priestess, would blank out her consciousness and let it be used temporarily as an instrument.

The very importance given to preserving the priestesses in purity shows that some consciousness still lingered in people's minds, perhaps from a higher age, that the purity of the message depends very much on the purity of the instrument.

The blanking out of thought as a means of allowing astral entities to come in had its origin also in ancient times, in the practice of meditation. Deep meditation is the polar opposite of a mental void. It is a state so intensely aware, so powerfully focused, that mental restlessness simply subsides. Today as well, in deep meditation, devotees invite God and His angels and great masters to enter their consciousness and fill them with grace.

I've said that no high soul would ever use a merely passive channel. Ask yourself this: what sort of soul would use such a channel?

Well, what sort of person would enter a house merely because the door was open? Someone, surely, with motives of his own. It needn't necessarily be a bad person. It might be only someone with a touch of curiosity. Perhaps his thought might be, 'Is there someone here with whom I can share?' In any case, he wouldn't be a person — to use the modern expression — with any class.

A pianist a few years ago claimed to be a channel for Beethoven. The pieces he played were, in fact, reminiscent — though only vaguely so — of Beethoven's style. But the people who heard him were not profoundly impressed. One critic remarked wryly that, if this was indeed Beethoven coming through, the astral world was having a negative effect on his genius!

Whom was the pianist channelling, then, if

not Beethoven? Some astral parvenu, courting an unearned respect? Or was the pianist himself a fraud? The latter, certainly, is the more likely explanation. Or perhaps the pianist was simply more open to the promptings of his own subconscious mind that he himself realized.

The subconscious does, in fact, play a major role in most channelling. One might even say that most so-called channels draw entirely from their own subconscious. And perhaps, after all, it is better so. Genuine channelling, if it is passive, is a dangerous pastime.

The best-known example of passive channelling is mediumship, which channels — or at least tries to channel — the voices of relatives, friends, or famous people to those requesting a contact.

Genuine mediumship is extremely rare. Usually, it involves the passive channelling of diverse entities. This practice is particularly dangerous for the medium.

For each of us is an assortment of many psychological traits, often sufficiently in conflict with one another to be labelled 'complexes'. It is no small job for a person to straighten himself out, psychologically — to become mentally, emotionally, and spiritually 'clear'.

Now, just imagine imposing onto that pattern of characteristics and complexes the pattern of someone else's personality. And then imagine a succession of such impositions, all onto the first personality. Can you visualize the havoc that could be wreaked on such a person?

Mediums often do, in fact, become nervous wrecks.

To receive the consciousness of a master into one's own consciousness, however, through deep attunement with him, is another matter altogether. A master is one who has transcended his ego-consciousness. He has become a channel of pure light, freed of any personal motivation, perfectly clear in mind, heart, and soul. Attunement with him, far from increasing one's own confusion, is one of the best ways of ridding oneself of any confusion.

Inner attunement with a true master is wholly beneficial. It is the first stage of *true* — which is to say, magnetic as opposed to passive — mediumship.

Sometimes a passive medium is in contact, not with many departed souls, but with some particular astral entity — never a high soul — who, living on the astral plane, can read people's written questions, or even their minds, and respond accordingly. Gullible people are greatly impressed by such seemingly miraculous insight, failing to realize that, in the astral world, telepathic communication is the norm!

A rare handful of psychic people have the actual power to converse with the dead, and not merely to channel their communications passively. Such people often have unusual powers of concentration, and a highly developed will-power. Merely to be able to converse with the dead, however, is not communication of a high order. It ranks among a vast array of mere metaphysical phenomena, and serves more to convey information than inspiration. The information given, moreover, turns out very often to be unreliable, for the simple reason that most astral entities are no more reliable than most people!

Remember, the fact that astral beings can do things most of us cannot, like read minds, doesn't make them necessarily wise. They have egos, just as we do. The ego is, in fact, an element of the astral body.

Astral beings, living as they do on planets

populated solely by entities with vibrations similar to their own, may actually be *less* conscious of higher truths than we are here on earth. For here, at least, we have the opportunity to mix with people on a vast number of different levels of spiritual development — not only with sinners, but also with saints. And it is possible for us, here, to receive the highest spiritual teachings, through the great Scriptures, and from the lips of great living masters.

Trust no channel that contradicts the highest teachings of the ages. Its source will certainly be deluded.

A few supposedly channelled 'masters', or 'liberated beings', have actually taken it upon themselves to correct the teachings of the Scriptures, and of great souls like Jesus or Krishna — as if the fact of speaking from the astral plane gave them access to information that even the great masters here on earth don't possess. Don't they realize that a true master has fully transcended not only the astral, but also the causal plane?

Please, don't be fooled! Such entities couldn't hold a candle to any great master, nor even to the lesser saints who have walked this earth in physical form. Were those so-called 'liberated beings' of the high calibre they claim to be, they would never in the first place choose passive instruments to channel their information to mankind.

There is a further factor that contributes to the inaccuracy of passive channelling. This is the fact that the channel himself cannot but be a filter for whatever flows through him. Only a true master — one who has risen above ego-motivation — is such a pure filter that his channelling is free of any such egoic intrusion.

The stronger the ego of the person channelling, the denser the filter. This is particularly true if the channel is involved in some personal way in what he is channelling.

Usually passive channelling, as I said, conveys information but not inspiration. It may even convey beneficial information. It takes much more, however, than information to uplift people spiritually.

Passive channelling also carries with it no sense of responsibility on the entity's part. It doesn't correct. It doesn't discipline. If its advice is not followed, it carries on in further sessions with perfect naturalness, as though the mere act of having offered a suggestion absolved it of any further concern in the matter. The entity is willing enough to share with anyone who will listen, but never goes beyond such sharing to offer personal commitment to anyone.

Normally, no question is too trivial for such an entity. A petitioner may ask it, 'Why does the point on my pencil keep breaking?' and it will answer with perfect gravity, 'Yes. In a past life, in Egypt, this person was a scribe in one of the great temples. He was conscientious in the fulfilment of his duties, but in his later years he became proud of his scholarship — so much so that Rapan-la — for such was the person's name — looked with fear upon any of the younger postulants who came to the temple to learn to read and write. For his fear was to see his own position usurped. That is why, in this lifetime, this person keeps on breaking this instrument of his scholarship, and he will continue to do so until he overcomes his sense of literary rivalry with others.'

Don't be misled into thinking that anyone who closes his eyes and begins speaking convoluted English is necessarily in touch with some wise being. Above all, look to the channel himself. Is his only claim to valid channelling the fact that someone, or something, claims to be speaking through him? If he himself is not a person who inspires others, don't imagine that whatever comes through him will be truly inspired.

The usual pattern in passive channelling is to flatter the people whom it addresses, even while sometimes pointing out flaws in others. It will make those present feel that they are being made privy to truths to which no one else has access. This fact alone, indeed, should expose the channelling as a 'power game'.

For a true teacher will teach those who have a need for his teaching, and will assume responsibility for teaching them to the best of his ability. Most of all, he will endeavour to help them not only with words, but with his vibrations, with his magnetism. Always, he will seek to affect their entire being, not only their intellects. He will seek to uplift them by his magnetism, thereby awakening their own latent spirituality.

That is why, when true masters want to help mankind, they don't stoop to selecting a passive channel through which to speak. They incarnate on earth as human beings, and walk and live with other human beings. They share men's sufferings, that they may show them an example of how to overcome suffering. They share men's struggles, that men may be inspired themselves to struggle — but in the right way, to victory.

They assume deep spiritual responsibility for those whom they feel divinely guided to help. If a disciple errs, they don't hesitate to tell him so, and to keep on prodding him until he overcomes his error.

Their wisdom isn't filtered by personality traits and prejudices of their own, for they have none. They have no personal likes and dislikes, no attachments, no desires. They are channels in the truest, divine sense. Nothing they say is ego-motivated. Their every inspiration comes from God, and from those high souls who, like them, are merged in God.

Most important of all, they never try to make people dependent on them for their channelling. Their students are never left with no other recourse than to come to them for counselling. Masters seek ever to make people dependent only on the divine within them. They teach their students to become their own channels.

And what more important message could they give us than this: 'As we have done, so must you do, too, if you would be students worthy of our ministry'?

CHAPTER FIVE

WHAT KIND OF CHANNELLING DO YOU WANT?

There are as many possible kinds of channelling as there are people. For it is human beings who determine the quality of any magnetic appeal they send out for channelling. Each of them has his own nature, his own special combination of interests and desires.

A few people, heavy with the delusion of egoism, deliberately petition darker astral forces to help them fulfil their desires for unearned riches, or worldly power, or revenge. Others seek to become channels for the ability to see into the future, or to read into the hidden needs, fears, or destinies of others. Some seek to become channels for nature spirits; others, to be channels for music, or painting, or literature. Some few seek to be channels of divine wisdom and understanding. And some fewer still seek to become channels of divine love and joy.

The spectrum is as wide and as varied as humanity itself.

An important point to remember about channelling is that not only does the channel's own personality influence whatever inspiration he channels: He also becomes influenced, in turn, by that which flows through him. In this fact we see a valid interpretation of the saying of Jesus: 'For he that hath, to him shall be given: and he that hath not, from him shall be taken even that which he hath.' (Mark 4:25.) For according to the kinds of vibrations we emanate, we receive in return. And if we emanate nothing — if, in other words, we live habitually in a state of mental poverty, apathy, and dullness — we release into the great void we have created around ourselves what little magnetism we may once have possessed — like a small planet that slowly loses its atmosphere for lack of sufficient gravitational attraction to hold it.

As we ask, so we receive.

An American army officer during the Second World War was posted to the north of India. Living near the border, it was possible for him sometimes to enter into Tibet. On one of his several visits there, he expressed an interest in Tibetan black magic. Perhaps he thought the subject merely a quaint matter of folkloric interest. Or perhaps he considered it amusing.

In any case, somehow he managed to encounter a man who agreed to take him to a gathering of black magicians. This person disguised him suitably in a heavy, black robe with a cowl. For he warned that, were he discovered, his very life would be forfeit.

It was dark when he arrived. Magicians were gathering from all directions. As they arrived, they sat on the ground in a wide circle around a fire, their cowls partially covering their faces. Their leader, seated to one side on an elevated slab of rock, began the proceedings by blowing a series of eerie blasts on a horn made from a human thigh bone. The assembly then began swaying left and right in unison, and in deep tones to chant: *'Yamantaka, Yamantaka.'*

The American at first joined them in what may have seemed to him merely a game.

Gradually, however, he found his thoughts becoming seized in the mounting power that was being generated by the chant, until he couldn't have resisted the others' fervour even if he'd wanted to.

After some time, a succession of demons appeared in the circle, each vividly personifying a base human quality such as anger, lust, or greed. Then at last appeared Yama himself, the demon of death.

Yama began a ponderous dance, human skulls clanking in a long garland around his neck. Gradually, the American, who by this time felt himself completely one in consciousness with the others, felt a growing power emanating from this demon that was reaching out in a conscious effort to overwhelm them.

Urgently, with united will, the circle then exerted themselves to the utmost to drive back this force and prevent it from overpowering them. Slowly, the demon disappeared. The power in the circle subsided. And the magicians, rising in silence, returned through the darkness to their homes.

It would be foolish to imagine that those men, in drawing power from such entities, remained unaffected themselves!

Playing with the dark forces is by no means the joke so many people — intellectuals, especially, proud in their twentieth-century 'wisdom' — imagine it to be.

I remember once going into a metaphysical bookstore that, as I quickly discovered, carried a large selection of books on black magic. The moment I entered, I could sense in the atmosphere of the place something evil and unwholesome. I turned at once, even though a sales lady was already asking me if she could be of assistance, and left the shop. The lady herself revealed in her eyes the negative consciousness she was merely there to sell.

Another time, after I'd given a lecture, a lady approached me and, standing before me challengingly, stared at me with wide-open eyes, and demanded, 'What sign am I?' meaning, 'What astrological sun sign?'

So demanding was she that I found myself unexpectedly drawn into the game she was determined to play. I gazed at her a moment, then said, 'Capricorn.'

'Right. What day of the month was I born?'

I wanted to say the fourteenth. But that was my father's birthday, so I thought maybe I was being influenced by that fact. 'The fifteenth?' I said, more questioningly.

'Close,' she replied. 'The fourteenth. But,' she concluded, 'you're good!'

'Indeed?' I thought. 'And good for what?' I felt somehow brought down by the encounter, though it lasted hardly twenty seconds. And I determined there and then never again to let myself be a channel for useless inspiration.

All of us have flashes of intuitive insight now and then, some more than others. And some make a bigger thing of it than others do.

You've surely had people come up to you occasionally, perhaps at a party, and, staring you in the eye, profess to see something in you that either you weren't expected to know, or that only you, presumably, could possibly know. Their primary motive in speaking, obviously, has not been so much to help you as to impress you with their psychic insight.

When channelling becomes an affirmation of the ego, the ego, which acts as a filter for the information it transmits, eventually becomes too dense to channel at all. Meanwhile, the very act of channelling actually lowers, instead of raising, the consciousness. For egotism invariably carries one down deeper into delusion.

People will go to great lengths, unfortunately, to impress others with their psychic ability.

I was scheduled to give a series of classes some years ago in San Francisco. Someone telephoned me to make a few inquiries about them. After I'd answered her questions, she asked, 'What sign are you?'

'Guess,' I suggested.

'Libra?'

'No.'

'Gemini?'

'Guess again.'

'Virgo?'

She went through ten of the twelve zodiacal signs. On the eleventh guess she got it right.

'It figures!' she announced smugly.

'Maybe,' I replied, 'but *you* didn't figure it!'

There is a story in India that some saint in ancient times placed a curse on all astrologers. Put this way, it seems a fairly sweeping denunciation, and hardly the sort of thing that one might expect of a saint. If, on the other hand, the man was merely commenting on a quality he'd observed in people with a tendency to probe, uninvited, into the privacy of other people's minds and lives, he may merely have been making an astute observation. For such people do often seem to be living under a sort of psychic cloud, as though their constant probing into others' lives had left them not entirely clean.

I don't at all wish to imply that everyone who engages in astrology or similar arts falls in the same category. I have known people with remarkable insight, for whom their art was a means of sincerely helping people, and whose own lives benefited as a result. It's a question of whom the person is helping, and how.

Is he merely serving his own ends — using people, in other words, in order to gain recognition or power for himself? Or does he see his science as an opening through which he can serve others? Are people the reality with which he deals? Or are they, to him, merely 'types', which he pigeonholes to justify his pride in his skill? Are people more real to him than his science?

An Indian I knew had studied palmistry in his own country. In America he once offered to read palms for people at a fund-raising event. A woman requested a reading. He inspected her palm for a time, then solemnly announced, 'You have two children.'

'I haven't any children!' she replied, astonished at his self-confidence.

'Are you sure?' he asked.

Laughing, she summed up her reaction for me later: 'As if I might have in fact had a child or two, here or there, but somehow forgotten about them!'

Channelling can very easily get to be an 'ego game'. Unwarranted intrusion into the lives of others, moreover, is no different, essentially, from the example given in the last chapter, of entering a person's house merely because the door is open. The difference, in this case, is that what many psychically inclined people often try to do is force open the door.

If you are interested in developing your ability as a channel, keep in mind that there are many bands of colour in the spectrum of channelling. I assume that if you were interested in black magic you wouldn't be reading this book. But even in white magic — attunement to forces, in other words, or to levels of consciousness that are not harmful, and sometimes even beneficial, but that are not of a particularly high order — there is a great deal of energy expended. Ask yourself: Is it worth it?

If you understand that you yourself will be influenced by whatever inspiration you channel, you will realize that channelling is something to be taken very seriously. It should not be treated as a parlour game. Too often, people try to channel as a means of 'seeing into' others. But the real job before us in life is to see into ourselves — into our own hidden motives and desires, and into the self-justifications we offer ourselves and others for the errors we commit. Our job, as the ancient Greeks put it, is *to know ourselves*. Channelling of the right kind can help us in this sense especially.

Most important of all is not to develop the gift of channelling for the sake of gaining power, but for the sake of expressing love, and in the process to develop our own capacity for love. Only by loving others unselfishly and impersonally, can you really come to understand them. Only by fully enjoying the songs you sing can they come out beautifully. Only by loving others and the health you bring them can you truly heal them. Only by loving the truth, as you lecture, can you speak with true wisdom.

And only by loving the light can you become a channel for the light.

CHAPTER SIX

HOW TO BE A CHANNEL

Paramhansa Yogananda's commentaries on the *Bhagavad Gita* are among the most profound spiritual treatises I have ever read. After completing them, he told me that his method of writing had been to tune in to the soul of Byasa, the author of the *Bhagavad Gita*.

'I asked him to use me as his channel,' he explained, 'that everything I wrote about his great Scripture would be what he himself intended.'

I was with Yogananda while he dictated much of this work. And I observed his method of channelling. He didn't sit back, close his eyes, and slip into subconsciousness.

Far from being unconscious, the state he entered was very much more than man's normal, outward consciousness.

He would lower his eyelids, go within, and gaze up into the spiritual eye. Stilling his mind at that point, he would pass quickly into superconsciousness. And then he would speak.

When he lectured, it was the same way, though before the public he had eye contact with his audience, and often gazed at an individual as he spoke words of comfort or advice intended especially for that person. If people complimented him afterwards on his talk, he would reply with perfect sincerity, 'God did it, not I.'

Before lecturing, he would remain silent and withdrawn, and tune in to higher guidance. During the lecture itself, one could sense that he always kept a part of himself withdrawn, consciously held open to the higher Self as it flowed through him. So inspired was he at such times that even the tones of his voice rang with the bliss of God.

What is the difference between the higher Self I've referred to, and God? None, essentially. It is God in us. For this higher Self (always written with a capital 'S') is not actually a thing, like the ego. It is simply an opening onto the Infinite. It is that opening through which God flows into us.

The lower self (written with a small 's') is the ego. This part of us is like a stained glass window, by the colours of which the infinite Light shining through man is transformed. Dense ego-consciousness acts like dirt or heavy pigmentation on the window. The denser the ego, the more both the colour of the glass and the light behind it become obscured. The purer the ego, on the other hand, the purer its colour, and the clearer the light that shines through it. If we want to advance spiritually, we need to allow ever more light to pass through the window of our egos. And that is what is known as channelling.

This is why, in channelling, we needn't reach *out* beyond ourselves. What we must do is go within.

Perfect channelling occurs when the window is removed, as the ego is removed when one attains perfect enlightenment. Once this happens, the sunlight of divine grace can flow freely through the opening of our consciousness, uncoloured by any human prejudice or other defect.

Paramhansa Yogananda taught us always, whether lecturing, writing, or serving others in any other capacity, to maintain a consciousness of inner upliftedness and attunement with God. I have found that this is the way to transmit not only divine inspiration, but even information that one doesn't yet possess consciously oneself.

When writing my book, *Your Sun Sign as a Spiritual Guide*, there were many occasions when the despairing thought came to me, 'I've taken on more than I can handle!' and then I would calm my mind, focus it on the point between the eyebrows (the spiritual eye), and pray, 'Give me the answer I need.'

The answer always came. In two or three cases I received obscure explanations, for which at the time I could find no corroboration anywhere. Later, however, I found them substantiated by writers who described them as having appeared in very ancient texts.

In this way, the whole book came to be written.

Yogananda one time, while writing, used the word 'noil'. Editors assured him the word didn't exist, at least not in the way he had used it.

'But I know it exists,' he assured them, 'otherwise it wouldn't have come to me!' He insisted they look in other dictionaries.

Eventually they found it — in a dictionary several centuries old!

It mustn't be imagined that everything that one says while serving, or trying his best to serve, as a channel must be God's perfect truth — even if that is what one is trying to channel. I remember a lady coming to me many years ago, after a lecture, and complimenting me on my talk.

'God is the doer,' I replied, wanting to give Him the credit for anything I might have said that inspired her.

'Oh — *really*?!' she exclaimed in amazement — as though to say, 'I knew your talk was good, but I didn't realize it was *that* good!'

We must affirm the reality, that it may become ever more real. The more consciously and willingly one lets God flow through him, however, the more perfect will be his channelling.

It is important to understand what function the human will plays in channelling. During one of my early lectures, the thought came to me, 'If I really want God to use my voice, why don't I simply stop speaking, and let Him take over?' I stood there in silence for at least two minutes. Try pausing that long, when you have a room full of people sitting there uneasily, waiting for you to speak! A friend of mine, thinking I must have frozen because of fear, admitted to me later that he'd become so nervous that he found his forehead bathed in perspiration.

At last I decided that the experiment had been sufficient, and that God wasn't going to use me as a passive instrument. I therefore resumed the lecture, seeking inspiration for it in the process of talking, as before.

A prayer that Yogananda taught us to say was, 'Father, I will reason, I will will, I will act, but guide Thou my reason, will, and activity to the right path in everything.' What he was saying was that guidance comes during, and not always before, our expression of it. In the very expression, we attract its flow.

Practice is necessary for perfection in any art. This is certainly true for channelling. The more you try sincerely to be a channel for inspiration, the more clearly you will find yourself being used as a channel.

I remember once, while writing the music for a slide show on Assisi and the life of St

Francis, thinking, 'It would be nice to have a simple medieval-sounding melody to go with the years of his youth, before conversion.' The trouble was, I didn't know any medieval music. Without some sort of model to go by, my aspiration seemed doomed to failure. But then I thought, 'No, if I ask Him, God will give it to me.' I got up and went into my living room, where the piano is located. It was as though an angel were sitting on my right shoulder. In the few steps between my office and the living room, the melody was already clear in my mind. Everyone who has heard it says it does indeed sound very medieval.

Sometimes, indeed, channelling happens without our conscious will, particularly if we have a clear understanding of what it is we want to express. One time I wanted, while creating another slide show called 'Different Worlds', a melody that would express the human condition in all its sadness and joy, yearning and fear, fulfilment and disappointment. It was a tall order, and seemed beyond my abilities. I kept putting off the challenge.

Then one day, praying that this melody would come to me on its own, I sat at the piano and allowed my fingers to roam about the keys freely, without controlling them with any conscious effort of will. Immediately, without effort, and without the slightest hesitation or fumbling, the right melody appeared. A friend present in the room cried out, 'Why, that's the *perfect* melody for your new slide show, "Different Worlds." It says it all!'

The conscious will is, in fact, sometimes by-passed while channelling, once one is open enough to the guidance one is receiving. Yogananda would sometimes remark, of something he had done, 'I didn't want to, but God made me do it.' It must be understood that when he said he didn't want to do it he didn't mean to imply that he resisted doing it, but only that he'd had no conscious intention of doing it. A great master like Yogananda is, in fact, so united with the divine will that it is never easy to tell whether he actually intended a thing or not. The ego principle being absent, even miracles occur in his presence almost as if manifesting themselves automatically.

I remember a garden party at which Yogananda spoke many years ago in Beverly Hills. Normally, any speech given at such an event is naturally kept light and inconsequential, perhaps humorous, in keeping with the spirit of the occasion. What was our surprise, then, and I imagine also his, when the words that burst forth were words of such divine power as I have never heard spoken, either before or since. God's power was present, in total indifference to the worldly expectations of man!

You may wonder, 'How can I develop my own ability to be a channel?' Here are a few suggestions.

First, keep your mind elevated during the whole time that you want to serve as a channel. Don't simply open yourself passively. Don't imagine that true channelling is something like automatic writing. Raise your consciousness in joyful inner expectation.

It will help you to concentrate specifically in the upper *chakras*, or psychic centres, of your body. In the spine opposite the heart, feel the power of intuitive love, and feel it rise upward toward the brain.

In the brain, focus your attention at the point between the eyebrows, that centre where the spiritual eye is beheld.

The centre of the ego in the body is the medulla oblongata, at the base of the brain. It is easy to tell when a speaker's energy is focused in his ego. Tension in the area of the medulla oblongata causes him to toss his head about jerkily, left, right, backwards, sometimes so violently as to make him seem like a wired puppet. When you lecture, or engage in creative expression of any kind, make it a point consciously to release the energy in the medulla and to let it flow forward to the point between the eyebrows.

If you are giving vocal expression to your inspiration, such as in teaching, lecturing, or singing, be focused as well in the throat centre, in the spine opposite the base of the throat. It will help you to keep an expansive mental attitude, and also to infuse your voice with vibrations of peace and spiritual power.

Before speaking or channelling in any way, meditate deeply. Calm your thoughts. Lift your whole spirit up to God and ask Him to guide and inspire you.

While channelling, also, it helps to visualize yourself surrounded by an aura of light. Expand that aura outward from your body, until it fills the room.

Second, give outward expression to your inspiration. Don't let it lie dormant within you, or it will gradually wither and die. Don't be afraid that what you express sounds silly — though, if it seems too outrageous, tell it to the trees; don't inflict it on people!

One of the most important principles of creative expression — which, rightly understood, is only another name for channelling — is at first to allow the ideas to flow without judging them for their validity. What this does is launch a flow of energy, which in turn generates magnetism (the stronger the energy flow, the stronger the magnetism), which in its turn draws true inspiration.

'The greater the will,' Yogananda used to say, 'the greater the flow of energy.' It requires a completely positive flow of will and energy, a strong expectation that one will receive the inspiration he wants, for channelling to take place.

An example of this practice may be seen in the charismatic churches: the practice of talking in tongues. Believers claim that what they are doing is channelling foreign languages, although there are two sensible objections to this claim: one, that the syllables used follow a pattern that is too simple and too repetitious for the normal patterns of speech; and two, that God surely wouldn't go to the trouble of saying things to people who couldn't understand Him. Nevertheless, there is something spiritually valid in the practice of glossalalia, as this practice is termed.

We might compare it to the expression of music, which is also, in a sense, a foreign language. At least, we can't easily explain in words what it is that it says to us. And yet, we feel that it expresses *something*. Moreover, by expressing ourselves musically we open ourselves to more and more sophisticated musical expression — a thing we would never do if we remained silent in embarrassment. By singing out our gladness, moreover, we ourselves become more perfectly joyful.

Remember, however, the higher Self of which we've been speaking does not easily channel sectarian truths. If you want to express the highest inspirations, you will find your openness to them at least partially blocked if you enclose your thoughts with narrow definitions.

The third suggestion for how to develop your ability as a channel is to remember what so many who thrive on uncensored inspiration (including those who practise talking in tongues) seem to forget: *the importance of communication.*

The effort to communicate focalizes one's inspiration and gives it clarity. It filters out inadequate inspiration, but in a positive way, by channelling it, rather than by blocking its flow with nay-saying. Instead of discouraging ideas with such thoughts as, 'You can't do that!' it says, 'Well, let's see how we might make that happen.'

When comunicating with others, don't try to reach them only at the level of the conscious mind — whether your own or theirs. Try to tune in to their higher Self, and not only to your own. Speak to them at their highest level. You will find your communication with them becoming much deeper and clearer.

Always be humble. Never think, 'I'm channelling, so people must accept what I say as the perfect truth.' The more you think this way, the less perfect a channel you will become. But the more you remain humble, the more freely the divine forces will be able to flow through you.

Humility, remember, is not self-deprecation. It is perfect self-honesty. In complete truthfulness you will always find your best guarantee in channelling.

Never channel to impress or to exert power

over others, but always and purely as a service to them.

Remember, too, the vibrations of what you channel are more important than the specific forms your inspiration takes.

Above all, finally, remember these words of Paramhansa Yogananda's: 'The instrument is blessed by what passes through it.'